# Selena Gomez Revealed: An In-Depth Look into the Life of One of Today's Biggest Stars

# Contents

# Introduction

Children all over the world grow up poor, hungry, and face incredible odds on their path to success. Many of these children are known for perseverance, strength, and courage. Yet, what sets these children apart from others in their circumstances who want the very same thing—a decent life with which the idea of happiness is attainable? What makes one child better or worse than the other? Is it nothing more than fate that sets these 'miracle children' apart? Are they just luckier than most? Is it truly about 'who you know' or 'where you go'? Those thoughts are vastly different than what children are taught in schools—that each child can achieve anything they desire. Perhaps it is the strength of this 'desire' that catapults a child from their dire circumstances and leads them to the success they wish to have.

Many people fail to realize how many children in this country go without the basic needs such as clothing, food, or proper housing. Some parents end up working two or three jobs just to make ends meet leaving their child in the care of grandparents or daycare workers. It is a sad statistic for a country that is supposed to be able to take in the "…tired, weak, and poor…", but the truth often hurts. Children who attend school without proper amounts of food often fail to succeed at school because they are distracted by the rumbling in their stomachs. Their brains do not receive the proper nutrients in order to process the information. Yet, something is being done to relieve these stresses. Many of these children have taken what they have suffered through and turned it in to something positive.

The sun is warm and the air is dry as it shines over the glass surface of the lake in Grand Prairie, Texas. Grand Prairie, Texas is located between Dallas and Fort Worth. Some of the most popular points are Lone Star Park, Verizon Theatre, and the Boardwalk Fun Park. It is also home to Lincoln Technical College. Imagine sitting on the shores of Joe Pool Lake with a friend or your family watching the bright sails of sailboats glide across the shimmering glass-like water. In the early mornings, people gather on the emerald fairways for a game of golf. Neighbors and families greet one another as multiple generations gather at the grandparent's house for lunch after church on Sundays. It's a town where Friday night football provides a place for kids to gather on the weekends to cheer for the team. The population is less than two hundred thousand people, but touts the title of the fifteenth largest city in Texas. Despite its grandiose size, it is still one of the biggest small towns in the country. On July 22, 1992, it was unusually warm and dry. Still, that day was not just about the weather. On that same day, America's sweetheart was born. After several hours of long labor, weighing in at eight pounds and eight ounces, Selena Marie Gomez was born to a young mother named Amanda Dawn Cornett Gomez and her husband, Ricardo Joel Gomez.

Ricardo and his wife raised Selena under their Catholic faith, but sadly her parents divorced when she was only five years old in 1997. Despite the divorce, they saw to it that Selena and her half-sisters had as happy of a childhood as they could provide. Selena's half siblings are named Grace Elliot Teefy, born to her mother and her new husband that she married in 2006 by the name of Brian Teefy. Her other half-sister, born to Selena's father, was named Victoria Gomez.

Many people seek to look toward the parents of a young actress with curiosity. Those people often want to know how those child stars grew up, how they got into show business, what life was like before show business, as well as many other questions.

## Her Early Life

Amanda Dawn Cornett married young Ricardo Joel Gomez upon learning she was pregnant with Selena at the age of sixteen years old. Like many young teen moms, she envisioned life was going to be this perfect experience complete with the white picket fence. To further understand Selena's mother's choices as well as the individual herself, let us take a brief look at her past.

Selena's mother, Amanda, was also an actress in her own right known as 'Mandy Teefy'. Born on April 16, 1976, she had somewhat of an eventful childhood as she was adopted. It is known that she has some Italian heritage, but her birth parents are not mentioned. In many interviews, she has always mentioned her pride in her daughter. Even though at the age of twenty one Selena fired her parents from being her managers, there remains no bad blood between mother and daughter. Mrs. Teefy has made appearances on Selena's short films including *Girl Meets World*. Though she gave birth to Gracie Teefy in 2013, Selena's half-sister, she did suffer a miscarriage in 2011.

Ricardo Gomez, Selena's father, does not have as close as a relationship with his daughter as her mother does. Much about him is unknown beyond a few anecdotal tales told to the public by Selena and the fact his ancestry stems from Mexico. Brian Teefy, who is Selena's step-father, is known to have a fairly close relationship with Selena more so than her own father. It was reported that during one of her breaks from acting and music, Selena sought out to spend time not only with her mother but also her step-father. This is highly suggestive of a close relationship.

In one of her many interviews, Selena divulged that she was raised primarily by her mother along with help from her grandparents. Growing up, Selena grew closer and closer to her grandparents. Her grandparents were the anchor in young Selena's storms of life as they have continued to this day to support her and be there for her through every trial and tribulation.

Selena knew no other life than one of struggling. She even recalls walking to a local dollar store to get dinner—usually macaroni and cheese. As many children of divorce, Selena grew frustrated as she got older with her circumstances. She wanted her parents together and could not understand what happened. In addition, she recalls that she struggled to see the light at the end of the proverbial tunnel. However, a benefit of growing up with limited means is that the child often witnessed the ferocity in which her parents worked to provide for her and her siblings which caused Selena to develop a sense of genuine appreciation for her parents. Her mother worked three jobs which often led to Selena being in the company of her grandparents more often.

It was on an E! Entertainment special in which Selena Gomez opened up about her parents' divorce. She stated that she did blame her mother, initially, for the divorce, but later deeply regretted it. She told the interviewer that she wanted her family back together so badly that anger grew inside her toward her mother. Now, however, Gomez defends single parenthood very strongly and is very grateful for all of the difficult sacrifices her mother made for the benefit of her child. Later on, Gomez's mother was asked about the events. She speaks out about the difficulty her daughter had coping with the separation of her parents. Teefy, Selena's mother, would also comment and say how her daughter would often vent and scream at her. As Gomez grew, she came to realize that any sixteen year old young woman would have struggled with raising a child with or without a husband. The fact her mother did both attested to her internal strength. Now that she is able to look at the situation of raising a child on her own as a young mother from her own mother's perspective, Selena has a new appreciation for the decisions her mother made while Selena was growing up. She also is a major supporter of programs that help the single parent.

Though there is not a lot of information regarding Selena's father, Ricardo Gomez, she recalls that he would take his daughter into Hooters restaurant to pick up women and watch the San Antonio Spurs basketball games. She may have only been seven, but young Selena took note of the fact her father spent half of the time with his child and half of the time with the waitresses in the facility.

Life, however, changed for young Gomez at the age of seven years old. In 1999, she was cast for the television show, 'Barney and Friends'. She played as 'Gianna'. She recalls that she knew nothing about terms such as 'stage right' or 'blocking' and that she learned everything from Barney the dinosaur. In addition to the wonderful opportunity, she met her present best friend, Demi Lovato. While the television show 'Barney' was often the subject of great ridicule, it was Gomez's big break. It was also where she was given a taste of what acting was all about when she grew too old for the part and subsequently was let go. Of course, by the time the show aired, Selena was in fifth grade.

Selena attributes her passion for acting to her mother. After 'Barney and Friends', it did not take Gomez very long to find her way back to the state again as a guest star in several movies. Starting in 2003 and 2004, she was given smaller roles in shows such as 'Walker, Texas Ranger' and 'Spy Kids: 3-D'. During her role in *Walker: Texas Ranger*, she played a little girl named 'Julie'. The plot of this episode was very intriguing. In this particular episode, Walker (Chuck Norris) investigates a shooting at a bank in which fellow Rangers Gage and Harper were involved in. Two of the robbers are killed in a shootout, but the third robber manages to escape. Later on, a guidance missile finds its way into the hands of a thirteen year old boy. What this boy does not realize is that three Koreans are searching for this device. The Koreans find and locate the boy and subsequently kill the boy's father. The young boy manages to escape, but not without the Koreans hot on his trail. Rangers Gage and Austin are the ones to follow the case involving the boy. Selena's character, Julie, is a small role, but one that continues building on her experience.

# Her Next Big Break

However in 2006, she received another big break in her acting career by landing herself several guest star roles on different Disney channel television shows such as 'Suite Life of Zack and Cody' and 'Hannah Montana'. In addition to the guest star roles and due to her role on 'Walker, Texas Ranger', Disney producers told her that she had potential to be a star and successively cast her as one of the three leading roles on 'Wizards of Waverly Place'. She held that role from 2007 to June of 2012. This role, which was depicted as a teenage girl in a family of wizards, was her big break and catapulted her into success that she never dreamed of. Her character was Alex Russo who was an intelligent young lady, but often a sassy underachiever. Her character refused to actually learn the magic spells taught to her by her family who owned a small restaurant in New York City. This show was very successful as it received many awards and nominations.

As a child and before her success with Disney, a young Selena Gomez attended Tavis Elementary School located on Pine Street in Grand Prairie, Texas. After that, she attended Danny Jones Middle School which was located in Mansfield, Texas. She attended until she was in eighth grade until 2004. For high school, due to her new acting career, Selena Gomez was home schooled from the ninth grade through the twelfth grade earning her high school diploma in 2010. Through her high school years, she began expanding her repertoire by adding a modeling and musical career.

Later on, she began recording the theme song for 'Wizards of Waverly Place' and recorded the song, *Fly to Your Heart*. Eventually, she landed a role in a musical film titled *Another Cinderella Story*. In that same year, she became an aspiring dancer. All of her achievements led to her award from the Writers Guild of America. The award was for 'Children's Script Long Form'. It was around this time that Gomez launched her own production company which she called *July Moon Production*. At this time, she partnered with XYZ Films and was scheduled to release two films under that company. The names of the films were: *What Boys Want* and *Thirteen Reasons Why*. This move not only launched her acting but also gave her a huge start in the music world as a music artist who recorded theme songs for the show. Much like her name sake, Selena who's songs she began singing as a small child, Gomez was now coming into her own professional vocal styles and loving every moment of it.

As all musicians do at some point or another, Selena began her own band. In 2008, *Selena Gomez and the Scene* released their first album titled *Kiss and Tell* followed by *A Year in the Rain* 2009), *When the Sun Goes Down* (2011). These albums got her noticed as not only a very talented artist but also an amazing singer. Word was spreading around Hollywood and words such as 'fascination' and 'universal' were being thrown around about her. Between 2008 and 2012, Selena and her band came out with numerous singles and a total of five major albums before going on a hiatus. The band was classified under a couple specific genres such as dance-pop, pop rock, and electro-pop. Through record deals with Hollywood Records, they released their debut studio album in August. That studio album earned Selena a Gold Certification from RIAA music.

Sad to say that after four seasons of paramount success and one hundred and six episodes as well as a movie, Wizards of Waverly Place drew to a close. This did not end Selena's rising star. Not only was Selena Gomez taking America by storm and becoming the epitome of 'the girl next door', her many roles as an actress and many songs took her to new heights at number seventy eight on the Pop 100 Charts in the United States. During the same time, she also starred in a Disney Channel film called, Princess Protection Program that aired in June of 2009. This film was a huge success for not only Disney but also Gomez. Over eight million people viewed the movie that Selena Gomez and Demi Lovato recorded their self-written song titled, One and the Same. It was released as a promotional single at first. Not long after her role in this movie, Gomez lent her voice to the animated film titled, Arthur and the Revenge of Maltazard. She was also in the 'Outstanding Children's Program' which won the series its second consecutive Emmy.

## Her New Man

In 2011, Selena Gomez and Justin Bieber attended the Vanity Fair Oscar Party. Already, rumors were swirling about a romantic relationship between the couple. Their attendance only confirmed the existence of the relationship. It was also in 2011 that Selena starred in the movie, *Monte Carlo*. In this movie, she plays a young girl who is mistaken for a Parisian socialite during a trip to France. During preparations for this role, Selena spent weeks with a vocal trainer to learn two different types of British accents as well as spent time learning how to play polo.

Unfortunately, life in the spotlight began to take its toll on young Selena. Not long after her break-up with Bieber, she reportedly checked into a rehabilitation facility in January of 2014. In an interview about her reasons for checking into the facility that took place in March of 2014, she states that she lost sight of who she really was and gave in to the pressure from her peers. She spoke out at the 'We Day Conference' in Oakland, California to young people. In her speech, she claims that she is not an activist. She told screaming fans that she was only speaking because she felt that her story might help someone else. She told the crowd of her adoring fans that she would rather speak honestly to them directly rather than using the platform of interviews conducted by media. Her words spilled forth from her mouth as she touted that the biggest influence of her life was her mother who was a strong woman facing unsurmountable odds in life as a teen mom. Her advice to the crowd was to always trust in one's self and admitted that it was difficult to do for her amidst the pressures of her daily life. In her speech, she also informs the crowd that while she has surrounded herself with people she was reliant upon for guidance, some of those people failed her. Selena Gomez managed to show the crowd that while she was an actress with life in the public eye, she was still just a young woman—the same as many of her fans—with the same pressures. She told the crowd that people were constantly telling her that she 'had to be' a certain way—nice, pretty, sexy, cute, and a plethora of other things—in order to market herself. She went on to say that those same people trying to tell her how she had to be were also telling her how to dress, how to look, what should be said, and who she should be. This is why she lost sight of who she really was inside. She stated that she began listening to the outside voices of others rather than her own inner voice. She became more concerned with the opinions of others rather than the opinion of herself. It was only when she realized that the only person she truly knew how to be was herself that she decided what she was doing was hurting herself more than it was helping. That is why she checked into the rehabilitation facility. Admitting to those mistakes of giving in to the surrounding pressure, she makes sure to tell those she was seeking to be honest with that she has learned from those mistakes. The speech was wrapped up by Selena telling the audience that her story was not about how *she* overcame life's hurdles—it was more about them. She implored with the audience for them to examine their lives as they were to see if they were listening to the outside voices rather than the inside voices.

In addition to discussing her reasons for going into rehab, she tells the audience that they are the ones truly changing the world. She says that she is not the one making the changes. She can only use her fame to encourage others, but the others are the ones who are taking action to change the world. She tells them that the most important thing is that people take the time to learn from each other in order to make each other better.

# A Fantastic Human being

Despite her success, Selena Gomez finds many ways to use her fame to influence to help others. Selena recalls what it was like to grow up with limited means. One of her proudest moments was being named the UNITED NATIONS CHILDREN'S FUND Ambassador. She does not limit herself to just the one charity. She endeavors to learn from each one and is thankful for the experiences they have provided her. Among those charities are among the following, but not limited to: Cystic Fibrosis Foundation, Elton John AIDS Foundation, Ryan Seacrest Foundation, Rosie's Theater Kids, Stand Up to Cancer, Alliance for Children, St. Jude's Children's Research Hospital, as well as UNITED NATIONS CHILDREN'S FUND.

Stand Up to Cancer was created originally to accelerate innovative cancer research that will get to the patients more quickly in order to save more lives now. It was founded in May of 2008 and since then has acquired over $261 million to go toward research. There are over seven hundred and fifty scientists working for Stand Up to Cancer who are running over one hundred and forty clinical trials in which over five thousand patients are participating.

The Cystic Fibrosis Foundation was created to support the families and the patients affected by cystic fibrosis. Cystic fibrosis is a terminal illness. However due to the research that is partially funded by the Cystic Fibrosis Foundation, treatments are being discovered every day that have been attributed to prolonging not only quantity of life for the patients but also quality of life.

The Elton John AIDS Foundation has taken on the mission to do whatever necessary in eradicating AIDS and HIV from the majority of the population in such a manner that measles and other illnesses have been. The foundation believes that by raising funds to create more programs and policies allowing the information to be passed to the general population about the reality of people's lives. The EJAF is among the largest grant makers for HIV research and education having raised over $300 million for treatment as well as prevention of the disease. Much resembling the personality of its founder, Elton John, this foundation is unafraid to discuss the difficult topics. The purpose is not only to educate but also to eradicate. This foundation is known for the following: working with community organizations to promote gay men's health, support young people in advocating for policies that pertain to their needs for better services, investing in improvement of testing, treatment, and care for those in impoverished communities, providing clean needles to avoid transmission through dirty needles, as well as ensuring that prisoners who have the disease receive proper healthcare in and out of prison, and making sure that people get tested. The base theory is that if HIV/AIDS can be treated, it can be prevented, and it can be eradicated. The biggest problem is funding for continual research.

Malala Yousefzai was awarded the Nobel Peace Prize after she sustained burns that nearly took her life in her native Afghanistan—where women have little to no rights whatsoever. Her passion for education has been inspiring to many people around the world. Many actors have worked with her in capturing her story in a documentary telling Malala's story. Selena Gomez was among these celebrities. Selena's heart for children was tested when she began to realize some of the startling statistics—most of which were coming from the Middle East and African countries. Over fifty seven million children do not attend any type of school in the world. The majority of these children, thirty one million to be exact, are female. Yousefzai created the Malala Fund to create change in this trend and eradicate lack of education and support the rights of children. In addition to Selena Gomez, many other stars helped with the project such as: Seth Rogen, Clive Owen, Orlando Bloom, Jennifer Hudson, Edward Norton, Shay Mitchell, Joe Jonas, and Martin Sheen.

It was in 2010 that Ryan Seacrest created the Ryan Seacrest Foundation. In addition to being an Ambassador to UNITED NATIONS CHILDREN'S FUND, she is also an Ambassador to the Ryan Seacrest Foundation. The purpose of this foundation is to support the healthcare centers for children in Atlanta, Georgia.

Since Ms. Gomez is involved in acting, music, and dancing, it is only fitting that she be involved with Rosie's Theatre Kids. Rosie's Theatre Kids is a non-profit organization that supports all of the arts. It was founded by Rosie O'Donnell. O'Donnell suffered the loss of her mother at the tender age of ten and found solace in performing arts. The performing arts has always been known as an acceptable outlet for children to work through the difficult parts of life such as losing a parent, divorce, or even growing up in bad neighborhoods.

Alliance for Children seeks to promote strength in families which directly impacts the lives of children. Statistically, children grow up with a better advantage if they have supportive families and communities. Resembling some of the work she did for UNICEF, her affiliation with Alliance for Children also sought the benefit of children everywhere.

Selena is also involved with 'Raise Hope for Congo' which is an organization that helps raise awareness about the violence in Congo as well as other surrounding countries. In the African country of Congo, war and violence rages as often and as easily as the stock market goes up and down in the United States. Since the early 1990's, war has ravaged Congo, particularly in the east. Despite its rich resources, it is one of the poorest countries in the world. Battles rage through many villages. Women are often mutilated, raped, burned, and killed. The children are forced to become soldiers in whatever militia wins the battle at the time—even children as young as eight years old. More people have died due to the war that rages than in the Holocaust. The biggest problem Congo faces aside from the war itself is that there is no accountability or justice for those who commit war crimes. The United Nations makes attempts at finding and holding the war criminals accountable, but the people fear the militias. Fear is a powerful motivator. In addition to that, these militias (even the ones who are supposed to be defending their villages) often gang rape the women in their village. The men in the militias have no regard for the women as they are completely desensitized to the level of violence. Attacks on the women happen nearly as often as someone sneezes, but access to proper after care and psychological counseling for these women is limited—if they are able to receive it at all. Many are shunned by the others in their villages and blamed for their own attacks.

The most lethal of these militias is called the Lord's Resistance Army, or the LRA. Led by Joseph Kony, they are notorious for being ruthless. Many children have been kidnapped by this army and forced to serve as porters or sex slaves, if not soldiers themselves. Many innocent Congolese citizens have died at the hands of Kony and his butchers. Kony is on the United Nations' 'Most Wanted' list of war criminals, but still eludes capture to this day. No one even knows if his motives are political, but whatever they are, it needs to end—that is the belief of many people including Selena Gomez and may have been the catalyst to interest her into working with the United Nations Children's Fund.

The United Nations Children's Fund provides children across the world, primarily in third world countries, things such as life-saving vaccines, insecticide-treated beds, mosquito nets, educational opportunities, and 'school in a box kits' which contain the basic items children need for school such as pencils and paper.

During her work with UNITED NATIONS CHILDREN'S FUND, Gomez was surprised to discover the startling statistics in regard to children who die every day from preventable diseases and preventable causes such as hunger. UNITED NATIONS CHILDREN'S FUND is an organization that provides these services for children regardless of income, race, ethnicity, or anything else.

The United Nations Children's Fund, or UNICEF, is an organization that was started in 1946 as a means to provide humanitarian aid to those in developing countries. Originally, it was started with the purpose to provide assistance to those who were negatively impacted by World War II. In 1953, it became a permanent organization. Often relying on donations and other contributions of that nature, it distributes approximately 92% of received resources to those in need.

What is most interesting about UNITED NATIONS CHILDREN'S FUND and believed to be one of the most important attributes that interested Selena Gomez is the fact that it operates primarily with a 'boots on the ground' mentality. The group does not merely 'throw money' at people hoping it will solve the problems. It sends people who teach those in need on a one-on-one basis how to take what they are given and use it to better themselves. The foundation has even established over seventeen regional offices to help oversee the 'missions'.

One of UNITED NATIONS CHILDREN'S FUND's most common fundraising events is called 'Trick-or-treat for UNITED NATIONS CHILDREN'S FUND' in which children collect money rather than candy from houses on Halloween to donate to UNITED NATIONS CHILDREN'S FUND. Over one hundred and ninety countries have a UNITED NATIONS CHILDREN'S FUND presence within their borders.

Starting in 1994, UNITED NATIONS CHILDREN'S FUND began focusing on the rights of children around the world. In addition to that, UNITED NATIONS CHILDREN'S FUND also partnered with MERCK and company to work on providing HIV and tuberculosis medication to those in countries such as South Africa where both diseases were prevalent.

'The Girl Star' project is also a project put into action by UNITED NATIONS CHILDREN'S FUND. This project involves documentation of stories about young women from some of the worst areas and neighborhoods rising above their circumstances and still obtaining education as well as breaking societal constraints placed upon them by circumstance and leading productive, self-sufficient lives.

Selena Gomez at the age of seventeen was appointed a UNITED NATIONS CHILDREN'S FUND Ambassador in September of 2009. She was the youngest Ambassador in the United States. Prior to that, Hayley Westenra held that title at the age of eighteen. Her first official field mission for UNITED NATIONS CHILDREN'S FUND is doing to help get kids things they need to survive and thrive, They would get clean water, food, education and medicine. Since becoming a UNITED NATIONS CHILDREN'S FUND Ambassador, Selena Gomez has also given her support to other UNITED NATIONS CHILDREN'S FUND initiatives including the Tap Project, the UNITED NATIONS CHILDREN'S FUND Snowflake Ball, and the ELIMINATE. Gomez was one of the celebs that attended the UNITED NATIONS CHILDREN'S FUND. There was two back stages passes that sold for a total of forty thousand dollars.

In 2008, Gomez's choice of philanthropies to be involved in would become the United Nations Children's Fund. For the first year, she was the national spokesperson for their Trick-or Treat for UNITED NATIONS CHILDREN'S FUND program as well as the following two years. She traveled around the world doing charity work for them as well as participating in discussions and events to advocate for their mission. In 2009, she would be named ambassador.

During her ambassadorship, Selena Gomez has made several trips including one to Nepal. On this trip, she visited the Satbariya Rapti Secondary school. She learned some traditional Nepalese

18

dances as well as learned some folk songs. While in Nepal, she met with other volunteers from other agencies to discuss and combat illness among children as well as their mothers. She also discussed some of the occurrences of conflict, domestic violence, and child abuse—particularly in reference to the Hapur Village. She also received the pleasure of having a skit put on for her entertainment by some of the Nepalese children about the importance of sanitation.

The point of her visit was to bring attention to the needs of the children in India. She described the visit as "devastatingly heartbreaking, yet inspiring". She hopes that with the help of agencies such as UNICEF, these children will be able to rise above their poverty and have hope for a more prosperous future.

After returning from her trips abroad, Selena came to the realization that she was beyond blessed—even in what she perceived as a difficult childhood. She realized the little bit she did have was still so much more than the children in developing countries had. Traveling to Nepal left her with a stronger desire to reach out to not only people who were less fortunate but also countries that were less fortunate. She reportedly was said to have told reporters and media that it allowed her a true perspective. She also told media outlets that she discovered that the worries people had, such as Hollywood's who is dating who, was extremely inconsequential to the things people should really be worrying about. Gomez also said that it is easy to forget how good those of us in America have it. The majority of us have roofs over our heads and food in our bellies. Even those who are homeless have shelters they can go to, and our country has many soup kitchens as well as programs to feed the hungry. However, developing countries have no safety net for their poor to turn to beyond the humanitarian aid of programs from organizations such as UNICEF and FeedTheHungry.org.

Selena says that even though her family has worried about her working too much and often points out her stint in rehab for exhaustion, she has gained a stronger appreciation for the opportunity to even worry about such trivial things.

Texting and driving as well as other forms of distracted driving cause up to nine people per day to die in car accidents. Over one thousand people are injured per day in accidents as well due to distracted driving. There are three main types of distracted driving: visual, manual, and cognitive. Visual distractions are merely taking your eyes off of the road. Such activities that a person does this is texting, changing the radio station, or even looking for something. Manual distraction is taking one's hands off of the steering wheel. Imagine what can happen in a split second that could have been avoided if you left your hands on the wheel! The third type, cognitive distraction, is taking your mind off of what you are doing—driving. Have you ever started driving and started thinking about what you were going to do that day only to miss the car that ran the stop sign? Driving while angry is also a cognitive distraction. Over sixty nine percent of American drivers admit to talking on the cell phone while driving! Younger and more inexperienced drivers, typically under age twenty, are at a higher risk of committing these driving faux paus. Texting and driving is shown to have the same effect on one's driving ability as drinking and driving. Over half of the students in the United States of driving age admit to texting, emailing, or eating while driving on surveys issued by the CDC. While many states have enacted laws in an attempt to deter this atrocious behavior, the effectiveness of these laws have yet to be seen. The reason is that police cannot pull over a driver without probable cause. Unless the person is being overtly obvious about texting and driving, it cannot be used as sole probable cause and therefore makes the laws against it somewhat ineffective. State Farm Insurance Company, ranked thirty-seven on Fortune 500's list of top companies, has made several commercials in an effort to educate people and promote safe driving. Selena was a spokesperson for State Farm Insurance to help promote safe driving and has appeared in many commercials promoting good driving habits that air on Disney Channel. With this, Gomez is becoming an international role model for kids everywhere. She had appeared in numerous television commercials. They aired on the Disney Channel to raise awareness of being a safe driver.

In addition to her philanthropies for children and diseases, Gomez was also a spokesperson for Borden Milk and Island Dogs. Borden Milk's trademark is 'Elsie the cow'. Island Dogs is an organization that sought to help dogs with no families in Puerto Rico which was also featured in a campaign print and television ads. She also participated in ads for Sears' back to school features for teen fashions. This piqued her interest in the fashion industry and led her to create 'Dream Out Loud'. 'Dream Out Loud' is Gomez's fashion line of floral and Bohemian style clothing made from recycled or eco-friendly material and allows customers to put their own look together to project their own personalities. This led to Selena teaming up with famous designers such as Sandra Campos and Tony Melillo.

In addition to Borden Milk and Island Dogs, Gomez also appeared in commercials for Sears, Inc. Her appearance was for back to school clothing ad campaigns. She also, along with Sears, launched the first-ever Sears Air Band Casting Call which would select five winners to participate in a performance for the MTV music awards.

# Her Unfortunate Diagnosis

Fame does not come without misfortune. In 2012, Selena Gomez was diagnosed with lupus at the tender age of twenty years old. Upon the discovery, she was afraid to let the public know. This is understandable as the public often tends to be critical of the famous if they show any hint of being less than perfect. It took her two years to come to terms with her diagnosis and be able to make it public even though she had a lot of support from family and friends. Still determined to not let it affect her life in a negative way, Selena refused for quite some time to allow this disease to stop her or slow her down in any way. Yet as time passes, she is beginning to realize just how much of a toll that lupus is taking on her body. She has learned taking on too much of a workload causes 'flare-ups' with her disease. In these flare-ups, her face swells, she has headaches, grows extremely weary very easily, and has joint pain.

Not many people are acutely aware of the disease called lupus or the effect it can have on a person. Lupus is an autoimmune disorder. What this means is that the cells in the human body meant to fight off viruses or other diseases actually end up attacking the healthy tissue in the body. In the case of lupus, it affects many different systems all at once. Inside the human body, lupus often attacks in a multi-pronged approach. As of 2013, scientists participated in a collaborative study on trying to locate a genetic link for lupus. Using a method called 'admixture mapping', they sought to discover a link between ancestry and lupus. Admixture mapping is simply put as the method of using ancestry-informative markers in one's genes to map out possible diseases. Though these scientists were not the first to discover the gene, which is called 1F1H1, they were able to show how one's ancestral origins can play a statistically significant role in developing certain disorders. This gene has also been linked to other autoimmune disorders such as diabetes. Through their study, these scientists were also able to show that there was a significant increase in cases of lupus due to a genetic anomaly, specifically in African-Americans. Mutations to the gene showed that there was an alteration to apoptosis, which is also known as the programmed death of the cell, inflammation as well as the production of autoantibodies. The next step in this study for the scientists is to explore how other changes to this specific gene affects the rest of the immune system.

Lupus is hard to diagnose as it masks itself behind other disorders by sharing symptoms. For example, one of the symptoms of lupus is chronic joint inflammation. Many people automatically think of arthritis when their joints swell. Arthritis is also an autoimmune disease, but is limited to the skeletal system. Another symptom of lupus is that the patient often suffers severe fatigue. Fatigue can be attributed to many ailments such as chronic fatigue syndrome, fibromyalgia, narcolepsy, hypothyroidism, parahypothyroidism, or other adrenal issues. A third symptom is that the patient can suffer debilitating headaches. Tension headaches, migraines, and even stress can be the root cause of a person suffering from a headache. It is also interesting to know that while stress can trigger 'flare-ups' in arthritis or even migraines, stress can also trigger 'flare-ups' with lupus. One of the most distinctive signs of lupus is a rash on the patient's face that looks like the wings of a butterfly. Though it is often the most common sign looked for by doctors, it does not occur in all cases. Lupus is the chameleon of diseases. There are a few people who are born with a predisposition toward developing lupus which can be brought on by medications, infections, or even exposure to UV rays. There is no known cure for lupus at this time.

Lupus' chameleon-like tendencies further suggest the fact that no two lupus cases are exactly alike. Some signs and symptoms may come on all of the sudden. Or, those symptoms could develop and worsen over time. They could be temporary or permanent as well as mild or severe. Some patients with lupus have periods of 'remission' in which they could go years without showing any signs. There is also one symptom that is called 'Raynaud's phenomenon' in which the fingers and toes of the patient will turn either white or blue upon exposure to extreme temperature changes or stress. Other patients experience shortness of breath or chest pain, which are two symptoms that people attribute to angina or heart attacks.

The cause of lupus is a direct result of a person's immune system attacking healthy cells. Though the direct cause of this attack is not quite known, it is believed to be a genetic issue which can be exacerbated by the person's environment. A person's risk factors for lupus are gender, age, and race. Lupus happens in women between the ages of fifteen and forty, but more frequently in African-Americans, Hispanics, and Asians. Some of the complications caused by lupus can include kidney failure as well as problems with the blood and blood vessels. Also, a person can experience headaches, strokes, seizures, and even hallucinations. The lungs and heart can also be affected. Often the pericardium, or membrane that encases the heart, can become inflamed.

Because lupus is an autoimmune disorder, people with the disease are often more vulnerable to infection. For Ms. Gomez, this is a major concern because she is constantly in the public. She has also been known to travel to third world countries where certain diseases such as Ebola and malaria have been known to run rampant. In addition to these diseases, those with lupus can be at a higher risk to develop certain cancers, have complications in pregnancy, and avascular necrosis.

There are many different types of treatments for lupus, but they are not meant as a cure. Unfortunately at this time, they are nothing more than a Band-Aid. Yet, knowing this, Ms. Gomez continues her philanthropy and charitable work, though she has traveled less. Selena is not the only celebrity that has been diagnosed with lupus. Toni Braxton and Seal also have the disorder. Though it is not contagious, it is highly dangerous to a person if not treated properly.

Currently, Selena has no plans to end her career, but she remains mindful of her health condition. Sometimes, she finds she has to be reminded to 'take it easy' sometimes. That, however, goes along with the energy of being young. When a person has lupus, that person's body struggles to identify what is a good cell and what is a bad cell. The 'flare ups' happen in waves.

Below is a list of some of Gomez's roles and achievements:

**Title/ Role /Year/years/ Episodes**
Barney & Friends Gianna 2000-2004 14 episodes
The Suite Life of Zack & Cody Gwen 2006 episode a Mid-summer Nightmare
Hannah Montana Mikayla 2007-2008 3 episodes
Wizards of Waverly Place Alex Russo 2007-2012 lead role
Jonas Brother: Living the Dream Herself 2008 episode "Hello Hollywood"
Sonny with a Chance Herself 2009 episode Battle of the Networks stars
The Sweet Life on Deck Alex Russo 2009 episode Double Crossed
Prank Star Herself 2011 episode Something to Chew On
We Day Presenter 2013 8th edition
The Wizards Return: *Alex vs. Alex* Alex Russo 2013 Special: also executive producer


**Films/ Role /Year**
Spy Kid 3-D Waterpark Girl 2003
Walker Texas Ranger: Trial by Fire Julie 2005
Horton Hears a Who! Helga 2008
Another Cinderella Story Mary Santiago 2008
Wizards of Waverly Place: The Movie Alex Russo 2009
Arthur and the Revenge of Maltazard Prince Selenia 2009
Ramona and Beezus Beatrice "Beezus" Quimby   2010
Arthur 3: The War of the Two Worlds Prince Selenia 2010
Monte Carlo Grace Ann Bennett/Cordelia Winthrop Scott 2011
Hotel Transylvania Mavis 2012
Spring Breakers Faith 2013
Aftershock VIP Girl 2013
Searching Violet 2013
Get Away the Kid 2013

Rudderless Kate Ann Lucas 2014
Behaving Badly Nina Pennington 2014
The Revised Fundamentals of Caregiving Dot 2015

Hotel Transylvania was a very successful animated film—one Selena enjoyed doing very much. The premise of the movie is about the daughter of Dracula coming of age and meeting a boy for the first time—something all parents have to contend with at some point or another if they have a daughter.

The television series as well as the movie of *Wizards of Waverly Place* is what Gomez is most known for with the general public, though she has come into her own right as an adult actress. Her mother encouraged her to participate in the role of 'Faith' in *Spring Breakers* (2013). *Spring Breakers* is a crime/action/drama about four college students who are trying to fund their spring break vacation. Rather than get a job, they get the bright idea to rob a bank. It is during their partying, however, that they are arrested and subsequently are bailed out by a drug and arms dealer.

In addition to doing the voice for Mavis in *Hotel Transylvania*, Selena Gomez also loaned her voice for the roles of 'Helga' in *Horton Hears a Who* and 'Selenia' in *Arthur: The Revenge of Maltazard* and *Arthur 3: The War of Two Worlds*. *Horton Hears a Who* is based off of Dr. Seuss' children's book in which Horton, an elephant, hears some noise from what appears to be a speck of dust. He eventually learns that there is an entire colony of microscopic people on this speck of dust and agrees to protect these tiny people at all costs—even the cost of being ridiculed by his neighbors. Gomez's character is one of the 'Who'. An interesting fact of this movie is that while Selena's animated character was the daughter of Steve Carell's animated character, Selena has never met Steve in person.

In *Arthur: The Revenge of Maltazard*, young Arthur visits with his grandparents over a holiday. While he is there, he runs into the members of the 'Bogo Matassalai' and endures a series of tests. Arthur passes these tests and is allowed passage to visit with these small fairy-like creatures called the Minimoys. During his visit with the Minimoys, young Arthur learns that the King of the Minimoys' daughter is being held captive by the evil Maltazard. Maltazard is trying to increase his size in order to take over the human world and

26

has tricked the Minimoys into creating a device that will do so. The telescope is eventually destroyed while Arthur seeks to save Princess Selenia (Selena Gomez) and is left trapped in the size of the Minimoys.

In the sequel to *Arthur: The Revenge of Maltazard, Arthur 3: The War of Two Worlds* begins fairly close to where the other left off. Maltazard is now human size while Arthur is still miniature. Selenia and Betameche accompany Arthur in his attempt to retrieve a potion from his home so that he can grow to his human size again. However, Maltazard steals this potion from Arthur. Afterward, Arthur seeks out the queen bee for the Elixir of Life which will also has the ability to enlarge Arthur. After a large battle involving the United States Army along with Arthur and friends versus Maltazard and his army, Maltazard is returned to his miniature size and kept prisoner by Arthur and his family.

In the *Princess Protection Program*, Gomez also starred in the film with her best friend, Demi Lovato. Gomez's character is the daughter of an agent who works for the 'Princess Protection Program', much like the CIA but for the protection of the princesses of the world. Lovato's character, the princess of a small island nation called 'Costa Luna', is hidden in the home of one of the agents—who happens to be the father of Gomez's character—in the bayous of Louisiana. Gomez's character, Carter Mason, is a tomboy who works at her father's cover business which is a bait shop. Though Carter Mason mistreats Princess Rosalinda (Demi Lovato, they eventually become best friends as she teaches the young princess how to act like a typical American teenager while Rosalinda teaches Carter to stand up to bullies from the popular crowd. The film is touted as a wonderful film about friendship and coming of age.

**Web/ Role/ Year**
Austin Mahone Take Herself 2013
Episode "Austin Mahone and Selena Gomez the Billboard Music Awards"

Selena Gomez formed a band. The members are:

Selena Gomez on lead vocals
Joey Clemet as the bass guitarist
Ethan Roberts as the acoustic guitarist
Dane Forrest on the keyboards
Greg Garman on the drums

### Albums released as a member of *Selena Gomez & the Scene*

Kiss & Tell 2009
A Year without Rain 2010
When the Sun Goes Down 2011

In January 2012, Gomez confirmed that she would be taking a musical hiatus in order to focus on her acting. She had success for her acting, though *Wizards of Waverly Place* stopped its run on the Disney channel. There were four seasons. This is when she acted in the Hotel Transylvania which is an animated film. She was the voice of the character Mavis. Her co-stars were Steve Buscemi and Adam Sandler. It was released on September 21, 2012. This film premiered at the 37th annual Toronto International Film Festival. Gomez also had a role in the film Spring Breakers alongside James Franco. The role Selena Gomez portrayed in this film was a more mature role than all her other work. A little known fact was that she had a bit of a melt down on the set.

Despite all that has happened and what has been said, Gomez started working on her debut solo studio album. The song, "Come & Get It", went on to be Gomez's biggest hit as well as one of her favorites. It became the first top ten hit of Gomez's in the United States. This was her most popular pop hit on radio as well. In July 2013, her *Star Dance* album was released. This became her first album to top the Billboard 200, and because of this, she hit her highest sales for her career. Her second single "Slow Down", however, failed to match the success of its predecessor. Throughout 2013, Gomez did embark on a Star Dance Tour which later became a financial success. Yet in December of 2013, Selena Gomez canceled her Australian and Asian leg of her Star Dance Tour. Gomez wanted to take a break to spend some time with her family. Gomez's debut solo album, *Star Dance* was influenced these singer's: Taylor Swift, Skrillex, and Brittney Spears. She now has a net worth of over sixteen million dollars.

Still, many of these facts presented can be found anywhere on the web. Everyone knows the name of 'Selena Gomez', but few know the real 'Selena Gomez'—her hobbies, her fears, her hopes, and the causes of her tears. Most everyone knows that she is an actress and a musician, but many do not know to what extent she has taken her musical talents. In addition to starting a band and performing music that soared to the top of the charts, this accomplished twenty-two year old woman has begun to teach herself to play other musical instruments such as guitar, drums, and piano. She also enjoys basketball, cheerleading, surfing, and even skateboarding! Most people would likely find that last hobby interesting, but it would not be considered odd to those who know Selena personally.

Selena is a pet lover as well, which may be obvious due to her involvement in the organization Island Dogs. Her four dogs are named Willy, Fina, Wallace, and Chip. Still, in her music video of her song, *Love You Like You Love a Love Song*, she had the horses in the video spray painted the color pink. This action caused PETA and the singer Pink to make accusations against her for the mistreatment of animals. She also enjoys listening to rap music, which is interesting because she sings pop. Another interesting fact is that she drinks olive oil to protect her voice. When asked about her favorite musical artists, one may expect her to answer that she listens to her own music a lot. Though one can be certain she does listen to her own music, she prefers for enjoyment capacity to listen to Fall Out Boy, Christina Aguilera, Vanessa Hudgens, and Paramore. In school, her favorite subject was science. In one of her numerous interviews, she was asked about what type of science she prefers. Her answer was that she likes physical science—learning about the Earth's layers. Though she says she is not very good in math, science is still a fun subject. One of the things she is particularly fond of learning about is about global warming. In the same interview, she admitted that the information she discovered about what global warming is doing to the fragile ecosystems has actually made her cry at times. Her mother and her have begun to seek out what they can do to help and encourages people to learn about it themselves.

Even though her mother is Italian, her father is Mexican.

Selena reportedly has stated that her family does follow some of the Hispanic traditions such as having a Quincenara and going to Communion at church, but her biggest traditions are Sundays after church in which her family goes to the park and has a BBQ.

Selena does have two half-sisters, but is the only child of her parents together. She does enjoy being technically the 'only child' because she does have her friends. Her grandmother also babysits for other families, so she always had children to play with growing up. This also means that she is able to be alone when she wants to be alone.

One of the most often asked questions actors or actresses are asked is what it is like to have to memorize a script. Each actor or actress usually has a method, but Selena says to interviewers or anyone else who is asking that it is much like learning a song or memorizing a poem. She just reads it over and over again until she is able to remember it. A lot of the scripts she reads tend to have things she would say in real life, so that helps, too.

She loves to watch horror flicks. She is not easily scared by a horror movie, but has stated she enjoys the thrill of seeing if it can get her to jump. Two of her favorite movie actors/actresses are Johnny Depp and Rachel McAdams.

Her on again and off again relationship with Justin Bieber has caused quite the controversy for young Gomez due to Justin's 'bad boy' reputation. When Bieber first entered the musical arena, he was known for being true to the way his mother raised him. However, he has since begun associating with other artists who have been linked to drugs and alcohol. In addition to her relationship with Bieber, Selena Gomez has also dated Nick Jonas and Taylor Lautner.

Some of the more intimate details about Selena Gomez's preferences such as her favorite color, food, fruit, and etcetera has been listed before, but knowing such information allows her fans to relate to her on a more personal level. Her favorite color is the color green. Green is a random color, but it can be quite gorgeous if placed in the right scenario. She also prefers pizza and pickles as her favorite foods. Could this suggest as to what type of foods she will be eating if and when the time comes that she will give birth to a child? It is funny to think that she may very well combine the two for a spicy and salty treat! Speaking of favorite foods, her favorite fruit is the mango. Though some of her food choices may seem odd to some, the oddest has yet to come. Selena Gomez has also admitted to enjoying eating whole lemons and even adds salt to them. Most people can barely handle a slice of lemon!

Her favorite animal is the tiger. While most people prefer dogs or cats, Selena prefers the more exotic tiger. I wonder if any of her friends prefer lions or bears…which brings me to my next fact. Selena is absolutely in love with the movie starring Judy Garland, *The Wizard of Oz*.

Despite her crazy relationship with Bieber, Selena believes in waiting for marriage. She has worn a purity ring that says "True Love Waits" since she was twelve years old. She still wears it to this day.

She also loves to draw and paint. In interviews, Selena has stated that she finds it relaxing—which is a good thing for her lupus. Stress often triggers or exacerbates symptoms in patients with lupus.

The book titled *Thirteen Reasons Why* is Selena's favorite book. The plot of the story surrounds a young boy by the name of Clay Jensen who comes home to discover a mysterious box on his porch. In the box, cassettes were placed which were recorded by a classmate named Hannah Baker. The odd thing is that Hannah committed suicide two weeks prior to the box being left on the porch. On the first tape, Hannah explains that there were thirteen reasons she had for ending her life on that day two weeks ago. As Clay continues to listen to the tapes, he discovers that he is one of the thirteen reasons for her death. In order to discover how he managed to find himself on the list of the fateful thirteen, he must continue to listen to the tapes regardless of how disturbing they are.

# Conclusion

Selena Gomez has come quite a long way since that five year old who had to endure the divorce between her parents. Divorce is hard on any child. Having one's father alienate himself from his child is also burdensome. Yet, Selena has taken these events and turned them into fuel for the fire that trails behind her still rising star. She has persevered through the trials of learning to be an adult while being famous, taking her fame and using it for more than her own personal gain, and has taken on many challenges in trying to change the world. Yet, she remains humble as is evident in her speech about her stay in the Arizona rehabilitation facility. She has lived and learned and continues to live as well as learn. Young Gomez has learned who her real friends are and is still learning to differentiate between those who seek to ride on her fame from those who seek to simply love and appreciate her for who she is. On top of that, she is learning to navigate the confusing events that her disease will bring about for her life. Lupus is no easy disease to navigate. Often, some patients must endure chemotherapy to keep it in check, but Selena still holds her head up high and refuses to give up. She has learned to take care of herself quite well for a now twenty-two year old woman. Selena Gomez has learned the wisdom that is often not evident in a person until their forties or even fifties. Imagine where she will be by that age! Still, her mind has not been wasted and her talents have not as well. She may have slowed down slightly due to her affliction, but it can be certain that she will always have a soft spot on her heart for those less fortunate than she has ever been—especially the children who cannot defend themselves.

Made in the USA
Middletown, DE
28 August 2015